The Bristle Cone Pine
& other poems

by Sheila Cudahy

Poems 1962

Clod's Calvary and other poems 1972

SHEILA CUDAHY

THE BRISTLE CONE PINE & OTHER POEMS

HBJ

HARCOURT BRACE JOVANOVICH
NEW YORK AND LONDON

Printed in Great Britain
by the Rampant Lions Press, Cambridge

The title poem and 'Plastic' originally appeared in
The Hartford Courant

ISBN 0-15-114185-1

First American edition

B C D E

Contents

To Valerie Eliot

The Bristle Cone Pine

In time of stress the bristle cone pine
hoards its life within a single line
of tissue and allows the rest to die.
So it survives for centuries.

In time of stress
we keep our life within the confine
of the heart and place all else outside
to suffer the diminishment.

We lie, embrace, limbs taut entwined.
Your face so close I cannot see your face
nor you mine.

In time of stress, in time of war
we hide, we hoard our love so deep
within our flesh

that we may find
we have allowed too much to die,
that what survives is spent
or rots at the core.

Plastic

A photo in the morning press
depicts a bag on the ground.
The caption states:
The plastic bag contains charred bits of flesh,
the remains of a man found bombed to ash.

Numbed by war news
I stare at the photograph of total demolition,
feel myself drawn into its remote, abstract space
by the bag.
The bag is real. It is mine,
one I am about to use
to line the can for trash.

I gag in recognition.
The burnt-out place,
the captioned epitaph.

The man, his residue
explode in my face.

Thrust

In time you lose your upward thrust
break down, are undermined.
Worm, infarct, rot.

Sense blurs. Slowly at first
extremities numb, fail to react
as if leprous.

The collapse occurs.
The parts outlive the whole.
You survive, some organ intact
but dumb, grub-blind.

You are
a snout, a sensitive spot
allied with lamprey lizard mole,
a brain in your belly-button,
        scar of severance.

You burrow, rut in
darkness, strain down down against
the weight of what you were.

The Last Late Show

Each night she watched late,
lived countless lives
with Bette Davis Joan Crawford Ali McGraw
in countless trials of
birth death love
televised.

She saw her sisters rise above
their fates and smile their tear-stained smiles.

No hurt, no circumstance defaced
their beauty, dulled their eyes,
those tearful eyes that were
more real to her than her own face
and now they wept with her.
She cried as the coffin dropped into the earth
and she tried to rise above
death.

Nearby her people cursed,
called her a whore, a sow
and worse under their breath,
heavy with booze.
She turned away, walked home alone,
four country miles in her best shoes,
and thought Bette Ali Joan thoughts
about birth.

  – A baby born dead, almost no child at all.
    Father unknown, then even less
    yet more than ever mine.
    My son, my son

why lost
when he had lived in me?

– Full term he went and of the nine
  he kicked for three.
  A good sign.
  I dreamed him Gary Cooper kind courageous
      High Noon tall.
  I screamed, bore down, bled, begged for him to drop
  and be,
  but at the crucial moment he quit.
  No cries, no breath.
  Curled up he stopped
  and that was it.

– Then Bette Davis Joan Crawford Ali McGraw smiled
  and rising far above me said,
  'You are the mother of
  the most beautiful dead child
  in the world.'
  and that was true.

Hard Hit

Wake up.
Jab, pinch, draw blood.
See whether or not this glob has a core
worth probing for.

Hit fast. Somehow, somewhere this fat cat
must possess a center
which once got at would elicit,
'Oh wow. that's it.
Good.
I shall hold together, last.'

Wake up. Time's short.

But what if the probe and pain reveal
nothing more than a stream of images spun
like a reel of film
before an audience of one
who sort of thinks, feels, loves
by means of
glob dreams?
Then what?

Not much. A mess; for to goad this clod
is like poking a hole in sand.
In the end all you've got
is softness which crumbles on itself,
has heart but no gut
to become other than one
who says,
'My God. I come apart,
rot
in my own hand.'

To Be

On Sundays the winter I was seven
we went, my father and I, to the Museum
of Natural History.

I remember the tall doors
and corridors into vast interior spaces
where rows of glass cases
stood like altars on stone floors
and in the lighted recess of one wall
a pedestal on which revolved
a stippled ball
under a glass dome.
A globe of the world,
ice cream on a cone,
or a big jewel? I wondered,
as the sphere shone and curled
slowly slowly on itself
in its own cool gleam.

Labeled 'Brain, Human Actual Size'
no hair no skull bone
it turned, veined rippled lobes
layer upon layer of glass-spun surfaces,
grey-white upon a core of darker pearl
before my eyes.

Later at college
I saw on a lab shelf in a cloudy jar
a brain afloat
like a clump of grey and matted moss
in swamp water.

I threw up in the lab sink
but in time relearned the wonder
and beauty of it, learned to wed
remembered replica to real
and to define the formidable mass
sealed in my head as my instrument
my given tool, mine.
In fact I was its,
its artifice.

And now later still I sit on my hams
hunker down in my brain
an ungrateful squatter
who should not complain.
It thinks; ergo I am.
But I want out of it, free of it
to play the sensate fool
to be part of a world
of the wink of a jewel
of a dream of ice cream.

The Christmas Ache

The wound never quite heals;
it grows numb, discrete
except for the Christmas ache.

When shepherds kneel
and wise men come
with gold and frankincense and myrrh
then she feels a throb
and seeing the star of Bethlehem
is quite convinced it winks at him and her,
at them as they Christmas window shop.

'Oh God,' she bleats. 'Oh, God.'
and he, 'For Christ's sake, stop.
What more do you want?'

Her lover vexed thinks 'mink coat'
though she repeats,
'to know and love Him in this life,
to be happy with Him always in the next. Amen.'
A childhood phrase learned by rote.

'You're a nut.'

'Go back to your wife.
It's the way I am.'

The lights are lit
on tree and crèche.
The shepherds kneel. The magi bring their gifts,
gold, frankincense and myrrh

and over all from the tree top glows
the Christmas star with promises
of love and life in perpetuity.
Oh, Holy Night.

He and she exchange the fur, the color TV stereo
but the moment is meanly knit,
their lives a burred abrasive mesh
which fails to hold the light.

'I'm innocent,' she pleads
as the loss aches in the old scar.
'You're a goddamned hypocrite.'
'You sure aren't Santa Claus.'

Unreconciled, they kiss.
Light bleeds from the star.
The tree assumes the cross.

Heroes of the Strip

Muckers drive muckers' cars
old Buicks, beat-up Pontiacs
with dented grins and eyes that pop
glaring from rusted sockets.

Muckers love their cars
purple crimson body jobs
sporting banners, racoon tails
and on the dash or back seat
dolls that light up, bob.

They go really fast
the muckers and their cars
blast off like rockets
spew exhaust. Muffler shot
they weave yaw cut you off at the pass

then white walls grabbing the concrete
they skid to a stop
and from the rear window a skull nods, glows
just to let you know
a mucker and his car are ahead of you.

They have the air of having been
and got through many a tough spot
on the strip. Saturday nights hungry for more
the muckers and their cars rev up.
Watch out you hard-assed Cadillacs
Jags Porsches goddamned foreigners
you don't know what love is.
They shout and gunning motors roar
into the parking lot of the Dairy Queen.

Recognition

From deep sleep jolted, shocked
by a strangulated roar
in every cavity and hollow
of chest and skull
– the sound of breathing blocked –
I freeze on the bed.
A pillow falls to the floor,
a severed head rolled in a sack.

Awake at last I see you sprawled
face up, as if beyond waking,
your mouth a jagged scar.
But your pulse is firm, your breath controlled.
A cough, a snore,
they reassure.
The familiar symptoms of a cold.
I welcome the curable mal breaking
the terminal silence at the core.

My Homely Ones

Dear runt, sweet awkward child, all my homely ones
marked from birth by homeliness,
even by ugliness,
I know you hunger to be beautiful
like the slender girls with smooth hair
the tall boys with new full beards.
Shyly you watch them gather after school.
They bunch together banter clutch pull,
relish body against body shoved
but no one touches you. Hurt you withdraw
into a cramped tormented loneliness.

Dear homely ones in time you shall achieve
not beauty – I make no false promises –
but confidence ease the learned grace.
You shall grow up, fall in love
and forget the pain you suffered when too young
you saw yourselves too clearly and too flawed:
the fat and mottled face
the butt too big, too small the eyes, the breasts.
Meanwhile you hole up in your rooms, blinds drawn,
and daydream such perfections, shining powers
beyond all reach of your ill-favored flesh.
And so your youth-time passes, sours.
Watching over you I grieve.
Not even love makes beauty matter less.

Critical

If I could strip my body bare
and find the livid sore
I could hope, if not for a cure
at least to be for a moment unaware.

As it is I finger the flesh
numb under the bandages.
The pain is elsewhere
deep at the core
and beyond the x-ray scope or knife.

Can no one see?
I am bleeding internally, vomiting pus
I am choking to death on my life,
listed as critical, put in intensive care
but there is nothing written on my chart.

I am near death of a wound
whose avid mouth
spits out my soul and guts
to the healthy beat of pulse and heart,
the wound received at the first breath:
the trauma, consciousness.

The Word Is Out

Chit chat.
Haven't you heard?
The word is out,
hoked up or understated to be kind –
nonetheless, it is bruited about:
you've had it.
Tick tock.
A meager measure of mortality
is all you've got.

You always knew that
but then out of earshot out of mind,
while now you are become all ears.
Tittle-tattle.
The creak on the stairs
the hum on the phone
the radiator's steamy gasp
all reporting one banality:
you're done for, hollow as a gourd,
dry rattle of belated prayers.
And the next rasp, the next drone you hear
could be the voice of the Lord.

The Pack

That summer our father was stubborner than ever,
he and the weather. No rain, no promise of it.
Drought clogged the sky with dust
and made the earth an oven
until it seemed the plains would split open,
collapse the barns and silos and reduce the house to ash.
He allowed it would rain before that
and worked all the harder.
But we dragged through dry August days
and in the evenings sat close-mouthed
against the old man's goddamned doggedness.

One night he said,
'Now let there be no rancor in my house,
not of tongue, not of glance,
and what you cannot understand, leave well enough alone.'
He cuffed at us with lean and sweaty hand.
'Don't sniff around like pups after a bone.'
Of love he spoke, of peace and tolerance.
We guessed that something big was up and nodded yes
to all that please sweet Jesus talk,
while in our minds we kneaded richer stuff,
the substance of a woman never seen by us
but sensed on sleepless summer nights
conjured up to fill our loneliness
and ease the raw impatient thrust in the dark,

We imagined how she would walk into the emptiness
of this divided house,
her shoes high-heeled and open at the toes clicking
against our ears
her dress stirring the dust

and the scent of her pricking our skin, burning our
eyes to tears
and the pleading look of her caught in an old man's
lechery feeding our lust.

Yes, there would be rancor enough.
(We could smell his mistrust of us.)
There was treachery and there was blood
in that kneading of thoughts.

She came, a loveliness beyond all we
had conjured her to be.
She paler than any child.
She stepping delicately in new shoes
excited our ears with her echo through these rooms
which hadn't heard a woman's sound in years.
How mild she was, soft as a young bird
and weightless as she went, picking her way
among our things long furred with dust.
The old man walked at her side
chirping in his dry cricket's voice
to hide his fear of her and us
as he talked and talked of love.

Dry days, dry weeks. August September. We forgot
        how long
a summer
engulfed as we were in the currents and noises and scents
of her which filled the air we breathed but could not see.
In the morning she was a step in the corridor, a sound
on the stair.
And at night when we returned dry-mouthed and sweating
the light behind her door
the sound of water filling the tub
and the click of her heels on the bathroom floor
left us sleepless and cursing.
Night after night in the squalor of summer
we thought of the well water easing her, wetting

immersing her pallor
white upon white.

One morning early
while we sat listening in the kitchen
listening and hearing nothing
suddenly she came running
her feet bare, her face wet with tears.
'Your father's dead, died in his sleep,' she said.
And it was true.
We found him lying on his side in the double bed,
his left fist clenched against his chest
his eyes fixed on the slightly mussed place
in the sheets where she had slept.

That same day she left
asking nothing, taking nothing
leaving us to our rancors and disgust
leaving us nothing of hers.

At the cemetery when the preacher spoke about
what love and peace the dear deceased had found at last
we almost shouted, 'No. He got them and much more
right here before he croaked.'

But how? What had he said to her?
What had she heard?
We had not understood and could not now
as we circled his grave like a pack of curs.

Blind

Startled by your sudden touch
my head jerks forward, jaws
as if hit from behind
struck at the neck
then comes to rest, cheek culled
in your palm's fleshy pouch.

You finger my face as a blind man does,
seek surfaces, nose lips chin jaw.
Does your touch see the hairless brow
beneath the skin, the eyeless cavities
and jack-o-lantern grin,
maw cut in the skull?

I know it does not. Blinder than blind
you are in your demand
for softness, fullness, ease.
You avoid the core
and as you talk of love
my cheek rots,
my head falls from your hand
and shatters on the floor.

Women's Ward

Women need appearances.
It comforts women to think,
'My legs are good. My eyes aren't bad.'
A woman can even survive on 'were not,'
on remembrances.
Her mind blurs
what it cannot blot out:
the figure and face she knows are hers.

Here we women are forced to give up all pretense
and to see ourselves propped, shored up,
drained, fed, vital signs monitored,
everything exposed. Without defense
we smell the stink, see the mess
even though bandaged, blanketed,
ourselves ugly in extremis.

Look there. That one in the next bed
with the tubes down her nose,
she dies gagged.
But Margaret here wrapped up in the chair
howls like a dog
each time she wakes up and finds she's got
her bowels in a bag,
wants to be dead.
We shut her up.
Maggie, pray to that saint who swings his head
like a lantern in his hand.
Put your gut in your lap
and praise the Lord for the next pain-killing shot.

Every four hours, a nudge, a jab.
Yes yes, we nod.
The stab of grace.
We slacken, sag, draw shallow breath,
become almost oblivious
to pain, disgust.
Yes yes. The needle is our God
in whom we trust
to whom we owe
the kind pretense of death.

Peace Games

'Come out, come out wherever you are.'
Who calls? What well-armed enemy
pretends
child's play
and peace?

'Come out, come out wherever you are.'
What false messiah offers you and me
his hand,
God's play
and love?

'Come out, come out wherever you are.'
Bullets, blasphemy.
The source and end
are the same:
hate.

'Come out, come out wherever you are,'
Our children call but we
who played and lost
the game
wait.

'You're caught, you're out, wherever you are,'
Our children shout impatiently.
'Peace must
be ours
now.'

Our children leave, leave us for dead
wherever we are and free
to believe or mistrust
their power
to love more than we did.

Dead Airmen

This is not our country, this flat place.
We are used to aerial heights and space.
Here all the trees are thin and small,
far from the sky and no birds come.

As strangers here we want to believe
a stem foretells the curl of spring
and daylight promises a pastoral
when trees shall bear us as we rise
whispering of leaves.

We shall put on the medium of eye
and see geographies emerge
from the silted hollows of our hearts and skulls,
green continents, white littoral
and tides once muddy in our veins
now running blue to blue.

There birds shall come, the albatross and gull
and in their flight we shall regain
our lives and see the place where we have lain
recede as sea and sky converge
in our steep suspended view.

Speculum

Nightly I look in the mirror and see
eyes nose mouth teeth skin hair.
It is a severe scrutiny,
an exchange between her and me
until she drops her eyes and the image blurs.

Though young I know the face we share
shall never alter, recompose
to be suddenly beautiful.
It shall remain – mine hers –
a homely face that would but cannot please.

Each night I carefully curl my hair
before the glass. The knowledge grows
from eyes to brain, spreads like a disease.
The mirror gapes and drains
my heart into her glacial stare.

The girl in the mirror curls her hair,
inspects her nails, her palms, the maze
where lines of head and heart draw near.
She looks at me and says,
I see your love. I see your joy
and promises prefigured here.

A lover who shall glitter in your shade
and claim it is his love imparts
great beauty to your plain young face
and boast his love protects
you from the critique of my stare.

His vanity shall move his tongue to praise
– not you, not you – but your defects
and he shall grab that spongy polyp of your heart,
squeeze it like a toy
until you cede him all our silvered space
and gladly put me to one side
for his grand posture and delight.
In time you shall forget your face
and so forget your place,
your role as shadow to his light,
obedient puppet to his pride.

The day you meet that image in his eyes
   – look at her, look at her,
   the primping foolish creature
   led round, decked out in gaudy lies –
then you shall seek me in your glass
to share the hurt and loneliness.
You shall search and find my features
no more pleasing than they were,
the gaze no kinder but now wise.

Goat Sign

Ardent goat
concupiscent beast
we suffer the sly smile, the stink
of you in heat
content with your goat's portion.
We envy you, sleek unshorn ruminant
we who barter, give to get
a modicum of love.

Our horny cheat slaps thighs, bares breast
in amorous extortion.
You lower your tawny head,
rut in the sun,
and wink above our loveless bed,
star-wreathed, ascendant Capricorn.

Risk

Go on. Complain.
Bawl.
Why not?

Invite derision.
Curse all critics be they pro or con
the works you craft with pain
to blot out everything
   that smacks of Beauty, Art.
Pursue the living imperfect thing.
   Love it.
At risk of fathering an idiot
   be true to it.

Stew

Little Zacchaeus, there. That's him,
   squat as a toad
up in that sycamore tree
   looking for God.
Who would have thought he
   would go out on a limb
for Him.

Damned tax collectors get their due
   and your purse bleeds
   when some hungry prophet stops
   for that rich bastard treed
like a possum ready to drop
   into salvation's stew.
A queer brew.

Blood dust and sinners' guts –
   said to be enough
to save a multitude –
   But we'd rather not
   taste the stuff.
   Not fit food
   for us.

The Guilt Game

Each night I count them one by one,
all those who wished and did me ill.
I check and find that none
not even one has died. All are alive and well.
Each night I forgive my enemies,
match face to name,
make sure each is accounted for
on a score I keep in fear of hell
and out of pride. N.B. Ur sin original.
In fact, one can't win at this game.

Some nights the count seems short.
I have missed some one,
forgot to repent.
But how when whom struck,
what face, name, eye for eye?
I recall only the gagging after-taste of hate
the knot in the gut,
the shameless intent
and guilt game lost.

A morning recount puts the record straight.
All sins confessed, all wrongs redressed.
Everything balances and I am in the clear;
but still the victims return, lay claim
to more and more kindness pity love
eroding my meagre store with their tears
citing old wrongs, probing old scars.

Mind you, it only goes to prove
that all along they were to blame.

The Presence

I am long dead, recently killed
in so many ways
you shall never comprehend it.
I leave you in ignorance.
Did your shot find its mark
or only graze?
You shall never know my end.

I leave you empty-handed,
no catch, no carcass.
The signs you follow lead
to coverts burrows nests
long abandoned.

Still you pursue me
here on the shores, there in the grass,
a presence viewed, encircled, treed.

I elude you in rivers, catch the wind's rise
and in canyons and swamps seek cover.
There are no waters where I do not bleed,
no air unsounded by my gasp,
no echo but of my running.

Exhausted, trapped, I give myself over,
shed my colors for those
of leaves, stones, shells.

I am recently killed, long dead.

With every season my cunning grows.
I lure you on, let you pass

to scan the fields and skies
where I watch knowing
that you not I
shall die taken by surprise.

Express

Heads bob above bodies compacted
in the battering crush
at the express stop.

Must be alert, keep my nerve.
No Paris metro this.
No petal faces these in this mob.
A burst of speed jerks them toward the light
where they freeze, sway en masse
in the curves.

Stop this train.
There's a killer in this car.
Murderer arsonist baiter of cops
I know your faces.
I've seen them before
on TV, in the press.
Every night I've watched you
stab rape beat.
I've seen you kill.
If I ever get out alive
I'll cut you down, and confess
Just to feel safe on the streets
until the evening rush.

The Lab

On the laboratory shelf in jars
they float like shadows in ice or mother of pearl
if shadows could be bright and cast within.
Transparent, curled they are lying
as in the womb preserved.
In the air they would disintegrate, go under.

They were forced prematurely once;
whether cut loose or spontaneously shed
one doesn't ask nor whose progeny they are
but wonders who bred, bled them in flesh
to leave them sealed in glass
where they wait to finish dying
long after those who plundered them are dead.

Cur

I can't shake the damned cur,
my faithful half-breed
ever at heel, sniffing the air
for scent of the end.

Quickly I do the good deed
say the half forgotten prayer
grasp the edge that cuts
and hope the penance stands
me in good stead.

I keep busy, on the move
but find I can no longer feed
the beast by hand.
It will have my guts,
go for my soul, devour
all I love
and in the final hour
leave me for dead.

Exits

How apt the exit
they chose
not knowing it
their final going.

The last rose
carefully picked
Rilke died of it.
John Donne
from vantage point of shroud
composed Jack Donne's obit
and Shelley's body on the pyre
rose in a cloud:
his elements
pure water air and fire.

Apt accidents. Luck.
They did not force events
but certainly deserved the break
they got,
not to end up like us
who want to find the door
that always opens out
and cannot.

We are old, unforgiving,
cantankerous as crows.
We hover, accuse our children
of attempts to cover up
the solemn requiems
they plan for our repose.

We disown them,
envy our heroes
and live contemptuous
of those who cannot stop living.

Contra

No yes
Fall rise
Go come
Our yo-yo lives
spun in the momentum
of contradictions
clash.

No yes
False true
I know you.
I have seen you snap
the back of the lamb
break the neck of the snake
with the same hand
and you have watched me plunder
a heart, take all,
then attempt to fill the emptiness,
give back more than I stole.

Yes no
Take keep
Wrong right
Together we bend to time and circumstance.
We break, we bind,
fight to keep from going under.

You cradle me to sleep saying,
  'We still have a chance.'

47

I people nightmares with your kind
then wake to promise,
   'We will make it make sense.'

You shove me off.
I let you go.
The odds are against us
who know as we must
that love is not enough.

Tourist

All is not well with me
driving the road to Syracuse.
The wind hums in my ear,
the concrete hums to the car,
   'Go home, Yankee. Go home.
   Here Plato came to grief.'

Along the road to Syracuse
contradictions confuse this tourist.
Assemblages of snow and green
abound beneath Mount Aetna's ash
and sunsets, dawns of sulphurous vitality
confound the eye, exhaust belief.

Where I come from I am used to
a world defined in maps
and proper postcard views.
Can Beauty be of easy virtue?
this Yankee purist wonders.

Seagrape and palm festoon
the curly chaos of the sea
and lure my eye from the road.
The car swerves. St Christopher disapproves,
looks surly on the dash.
Can Beauty be a tourist trap?
this Yankee ponders.
And the road croons,
   'Go home go home
   Back to your Disneyland reality
   Your postcard views of Good and True.

Here the knowing wink must see
more than it would.
Here Plato came to grief
and so shall you in Sicily.'

Soldiers

In well-greased vehicles we passed
down streets lined with ribbons of faces
dotted with eyes
just like in the movies.

We thought we saw our daughters, wives
in First Communion dress, in bridal gown
press forward, then recede, lost
crying in the crush of hostages
who at our coming shuddered and bowed down
turning on themselves as if they wished to drown
in the fullness of their dresses.

Our passage left them slack upon the ground
like dahlias struck by sudden frost
lying heads thrown back exposing withered faces.
We moved on in well-greased vehicles
back to bases, to home towns
down streets where our daughters and wives stood
with smiling faces, tearful eyes
just like in the movies
and we felt good.

Ambush

Sleep, love. Sleep late. Keep night.
This winter dawn comes hexed,
the sun bled white.
Hold breath. Press viscera to bone.
Play dead.
The earth is frozen, fixed
like a shriveled head in the cold light.

We are the last creatures left,
sticking like slugs to a stone,
hiding together on the darkened bed,
but the light finds you, creeps up
you, pries at the shadowed clefts,
crotch rib-cage nostrils lids,
and in a flash lays bare your skull,
slits bone from gut.

You start up, moan, sink back inert,
face forward as if shot
struck fatally, cut down
by sniper's fire, mugger's knife.
I grab, shake, pull you
wake you, hurt and shrieking back to life
at dawn.

The Hour

This is the hour of rancor and contempt.
The outer edges yield, the rot attempts the core.
This is the reason of declines and falls.
Few break the silence of the dead
to explain what went awry;
what failure of nerve or faith or love.
Few survive the attrition
and can be heard to reason above
the barbarous grunt, the hysterical cry.
Our fathers and our children call
their sins upon our heads.
Bad losers all, exeunt without contrition.

Barbarian

Remember, primate carnivore,
Praxiteles redeemed you once,
set you in delicate deliberate stance
to dream a marble permanence
although you saw within the stone
the forms of arrowhead and knife
honed fine to gore, dismember, kill.

Barbarian, wait.
Praxiteles redeems you still.
The legless torso, mutilated face
which in flesh decays
in stone survives renews itself
to fill the vacancies of light and space
with its ideal completion.

You stand amazed
and for a moment share the pose
sense the pain and horrible depletion
the stone knows it cannot stay.

You strike again and again
until the marble shatters.
Now you are alone
become a shoddy thing
hair patches, coarse skin
flesh slack, memory blurred.
A squatter.

At times in the ruins you hear
some obdurate presence stir,
crawl like a cripple up the acropolis

clutching at bits of marble quartz obsidian.
In fear you grab a stone, pointed sharp-edged
and mumble, whine, insist,
   'Praxiteles is dead.'
You have the final word.
The last fragment crumbles.

Swings

The cold hard drive of children on swings.
'Higher, push us higher,' they cry
humping then snapping their backs,
bearing down on the slatted seats.

'Harder, push harder.'

They strain against the weight and slack
pumping their arms like stunted wings
working the winter air with their feet.

We give a final shove and step aside
as they released begin to rise,
red parkas pressed against their chests,
scarves, hood awry,
each on his own
aiming to sound the drum of the sky
    to bound off the rim of the sun.
Bright knots of energy on pendulums
striving to over-reach the arc
driving to make the circle complete.
But no, it can't be done.
The swings resist the steep ascent.
The earth pulls,
we pull against their flight.

'Enough, enough. It will soon be dark.'

They refuse to listen.

Another passage comet-swift.

'Time's up. Time's up, so come.'

Losing speed and height they drift
without momentum
until they slump, strength spent, immobilized.
And though our kiss welcomes, is tender
their eyes glisten like wet cinders
and they will not smile once home.

Severance

Let us part
Bring about annihilations
Wish me gone
Wish you alone
Make two of one again.

But will cannot cut out
so much of self, strike at such depths
of mutual being without
a fatal mutilation.

The wish poisons the heart
to hallucinate
seek pain
live death
love hate.

Cold

We willed cold, chose it over heat,
made mind a bitter place
and shed a skin of ice upon the snow.

With fists iced slick as skulls
we blocked all passes of retreat
all areas of compromise.

Now all that we and winter froze,
the weapons footprints droppings blood
no warmth of spring annuls.

Now the ice skin grows
like cataracts upon our eyes
and blinds us to the strength of those
who come unarmed to trace
signs of peace in the intractable mud.

Peace March

The sabbath sun draws blisters, blood.
The road sweats tar and in the slick
some animal is mashed car by car,
fur flesh crushed in summer traffic.

We hug the side of the road
carry our placards: End the War
Peace now.
We camp on the grass in the shade
and talk of war, the dead, the prisoners.
A sudden ruddiness denudes the green.
The sun invades the spot
where they got theirs
as they got them
all turning the grass bloody.
Stop the War
Peace.
The march begins, then stalls.
Somewhere up ahead
crowds soldiers police.
Someone falls.

Someone reads a list of the dead.
The body count includes chickens and cows.
Rest in peace.
Someone demands immediate release
of all prisoners.
Stop the War.
The crowd shouts, cheers.
The air stinks from the heat and the cars.
'Peace Nicks,'

the crowd jeers, taunts.
Sweat stings our eyes.
We are afraid.
The guardsmen are afraid.
Sweat stains their shirts.
We sweat a common fear
of hurt and death no one wants.